$\underline{40}$
DEAL WITH IT!

By
JAN KING

Illustrated by
CHARLES GOLL

CCC PUBLICATIONS

Published by

CCC Publications
9725 Lurline Avenue
Chatsworth, CA 91311

Manufactured in the United States of America
Cover © 1997 CCC Publications
Interior illustrations © 1997 CCC Publications
Cover & Interior art by Charles Goll
Cover / Interior production by Oasis Graphics
ISBN: 1-57644-038-9

If your local bookstore is out of stock, copies of this book may be obtained by mailing check or money order for $5.95 per book (plus $2.50 to cover postage and handling) to:
CCC Publications; 9725 Lurline Avenue, Chatsworth, CA 91311

Pre-publication Edition - 1/97   Third Printing 11/98
First Printing - 7/97
Second Printing - 2/98

"40"
MEANS...

YOU SHOULD HAVE LEARNED BY NOW THAT YOU'RE NEVER TOO OLD TO PRACTICE SAFE SEX!

**YOUR DAUGHTER'S PROM GOWN LOOKS LIKE WHAT YOU WORE
UNDERNEATH YOURS!**

YOU WILL HAVE TO LEARN HOW TO DEAL CALMLY AND SENSIBLY
WITH OUTRAGEOUS TEENAGE FADS.

A MOTHER'S WORST NIGHTMARE: THE "CO-ED" DORM.

GETTING TO ATTEND THE BIGGEST COMEDY SHOW ON EARTH—
YOUR HIGH SCHOOL REUNION.

YOU'RE STILL TRYING TO HIDE YOUR BAD HABITS FROM YOUR KIDS.

YOU'RE STILL GETTING SUCKERED IN BY YOUR KID'S LAME PROMISES.

YOU WILL HAVE TO INSTITUTE AND ENFORCE THE "FASHION HOUSE ARREST" RULE.

YOUR BRIDGE CLUB GETS A "GROUP RATE" ON FACELIFTS.

YOU'RE EATING SO MUCH BRAN AND FIBER YOU HAVE TO INSTALL A SEAT BELT ON YOUR JOHN.

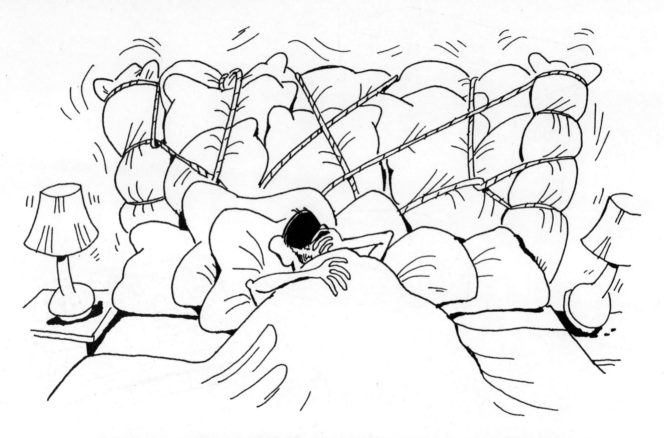

"SAFE SEX" MEANS EXTRA PADDING ON THE HEADBOARD.

KA-CHUNK

THE ONLY "BUNS OF STEEL" YOU'LL EVER GET ARE THE KIND FROM YOUR OVEN.

YOU DISCOVER THE "HAIR CLUB FOR MEN."

IT GETS HARDER AND HARDER TO OUTSMART YOUR HUSBAND ANYMORE.

THIS IS YOUR IDEA OF "POWERWALKING..."

EVERY BIRTHDAY LUNCHEON YOUR GIRLFRIENDS GIVE YOU FROM NOW ON WILL FEATURE A MALE STRIPPER.

THE FEAR OF WRINKLES RULES!

YOU GO OVERBOARD IN YOUR QUEST TO INFUSE NEW ENERGY
INTO YOUR SEX LIFE.

YOU TAKE YOUR <u>MEXICAN</u> WITH <u>MAALOX</u>.

<u>MORE</u> ISN'T NECESSARILY BETTER.

YOU'D BETTER FOREGO TRYING POSITIONS FROM THE KAMA SUTRA.

YOU INSTITUTE THE WEEKLY "GRAY HAIR ALERT" RITUAL.

TRANSPLANTS HAPPEN.

YOUR BRA SIZE GOES FROM A 34-C TO A 36-LONG.

YOU SURPRISE YOUR HUSBAND WITH THE NEW $5000 YOU!

YOU FIND THAT YOU ARE BECOMING A VICTIM OF YOUR OWN HORMONES.

TRYING ON BATHING SUITS TRIGGERS AN ACUTE <u>LIFE OR DEATH</u> DRAMA.

YOU'RE SO OUT OF IT, YOU THINK "SALSA" ONLY REFERS TO SOMETHING EDIBLE.

YOU ARE BEGINNING TO DELIVER THOSE SAME DREADED SERMONS
YOUR OWN DAD GAVE TO YOU.

EXHIBITIONISM IS JUST A DISTANT MEMORY.

YOU'RE CONVINCED YOUR KIDS HAVE STARTED SPEAKING IN FOREIGN TONGUES.

YOUR GUMS AND HAIRLINE ARE RECEDING AT THE SAME RATE.

YOUR "PERSONAL GROOMER" COMES WITH IT'S OWN 3HP
KICK-START ENGINE.

YOU HAVEN'T A <u>CLUE</u> WHO OR WHAT "HOOTIE AND THE BLOWFISH" ARE.

FOR YOUR OWN GOOD, YOU SHOULD <u>NEVER</u> VISIT YOUR SON'S FRATERNITY HOUSE WITHOUT FIRST GIVING HIM A 6 HOUR WARNING.

A "FOOT FETISH" MEANS AN OBSESSION WITH DR. SCHOLL.

NEW YEAR'S EVE JUST ISN'T WHAT IT USED TO BE.

YOUR LIFE BECOMES ONE FAD DIET AFTER ANOTHER.

<u>NOBODY</u> CAN EAT <u>ANYTHING</u> ANYMORE.

LEAKY BLADDERS HAPPEN!

YOUR "ROMANTIC DINNER CONVERSATIONS" HAVE BECOME DISCUSSIONS INVOLVING THE STATE OF YOUR BOWELS.

YOUR KIDS ARE HIGHLY AMUSED BY YOUR QUEST TO STAY YOUNG.

YOU DON'T THINK TWICE ANYMORE ABOUT VOICING AN
UNPOPULAR OPINION.

THE DISCOVERY OF "UNDERARM JIGGLE" WILL DEMAND
IMMEDIATE CHANGES IN YOUR LIFESTYLE.

YOU HAVE ELEVATED THE PRACTICE OF "DENIAL" TO NEW HEIGHTS.

YOU'VE LEARNED TO DEMONSTRATE YOUR DISLIKE FOR PRICEY, ROMANTIC RESTAURANTS IN <u>NEW AND CREATIVE</u> WAYS.

YOU WILL REFUSE TO FALL VICTIM TO THE "EMPTY NEST SYNDROME."

YOU'VE FINALLY MASTERED THE ART OF TELLING THE TRUTH WITHOUT GETTING CLOBBERED.

CELLULITE HAPPENS!

THOSE FAMILY REUNIONS WILL REQUIRE EXTRA MEDICATION.

YOU'VE DISCOVERED THE ONE MOTIVATING FACTOR THAT GETS YOU TO THE GYM.

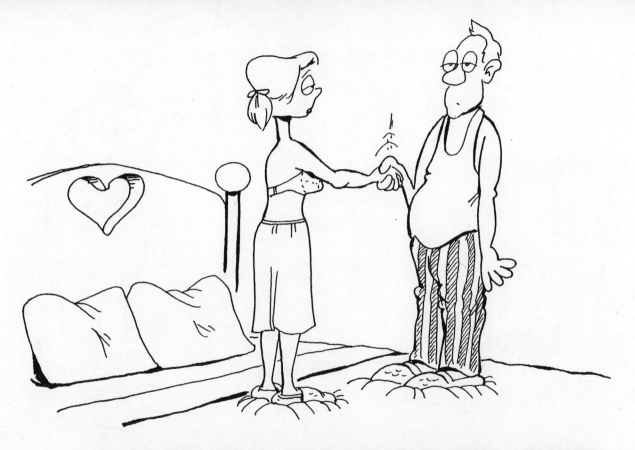

YOU ARE STILL CAPABLE OF HAVING FOREPLAY, <u>BUT</u>, IT REQUIRES ENERGY CONSERVING TECHNIQUES.

THE ONLY EXERCISE YOU'RE EVER GOING TO HAVE IS THE "EXERCISE IN FUTILITY."

MIDLIFE CRISIS HAPPENS!!

YOU DREAM ABOUT A JOB THAT HAS NO PRESSURE, PAYS IN CASH, AND GIVES YOU IMMEDIATE GRATIFICATION.

YOU HAVE JOINED THE RANKS OF THE "CHOLESTEROLLY OBSESSIVE."

YOUR "CAST-IRON STOMACH" HAS SUFFERED SERIOUS MELTDOWN.

YOU ARE STILL PAYING THE PRICE FOR NOT TAKING THE TIME TO READ INSTRUCTIONS.

YOU'RE FEELING DESPERATE ABOUT LOSING THE EXCITEMENT YOU ONCE HAD IN YOUR SEX LIFE.

YOUR "BIRTHDAY CELEBRATIONS" HAVE TURNED INTO EVENTS WHICH COULD BE NICKNAMED "THE GREAT DEPRESSION."

TITLES BY CCC PUBLICATIONS

Blank Books ($ 3.99)
SEX AFTER BABY
SEX AFTER 30
SEX AFTER 40
SEX AFTER 50

Retail $4.95 – $4.99
30 – DEAL WITH IT!
40 – DEAL WITH IT!
50 – DEAL WITH IT!
60 – DEAL WITH IT!
RETIRED – DEAL WITH IT!
 "?" book
POSITIVELY PREGNANT
CAN SEX IMPROVE YOUR GOLF?
THE COMPLETE BOOGER BOOK
FLYING FUNNIES
MARITAL BLISS & OXYMORONS
THE VERY VERY SEXY ADULT DOT-TO-DOT BOOK
THE DEFINITIVE FART BOOK
THE COMPLETE WIMP'S GUIDE TO SEX
THE CAT OWNER'S SHAPE UP MANUAL
THE OFFICE FROM HELL
FITNESS FANATICS
YOUNGER MEN ARE BETTER THAN RETIN-A
BUT OSSIFER, IT'S NOT MY FAULT
YOU KNOW YOU'RE AN OLD FART WHEN...
1001 WAYS TO PROCRASTINATE
HORMONES FROM HELL II
SHARING THE ROAD WITH IDIOTS
THE GREATEST ANSWERING MACHINE MESSAGES
WHAT DO WE DO NOW??
HOW TO TALK YOU WAY OUT OF A TRAFFIC TICKET
THE BOTTOM HALF

LIFE'S MOST EMBARRASSING MOMENTS
HOW TO ENTERTAIN PEOPLE YOU HATE
YOUR GUIDE TO CORPORATE SURVIVAL
THE SUPERIOR PERSON'S GUIDE
GIFTING RIGHT
NO HANG -UPS (Volumes I, II & III – $ 3.95ea.)
TOTALLY OUTRAGEOUS BUMPER-SNICKERS ($ 2.95)

Retail $5.95
SINGLE WOMEN VS. MARRIED WOMEN
TAKE A WOMAN'S WORD FOR IT
SEXY CROTCHWORD PUZZLES
SO, YOU'RE GETTING MARRIED
YOU KNOW HE'S A WOMANIZING SLIMEBALL WHEN...
GETTING OLD SUCKS
WHY GOD MAKES BALD GUYS
OH BABY!
PMS CRAZED: TOUCH ME AND I'LL KILL YOU!
OVER THE HILL– DEAL WITH IT!
WHY MEN ARE CLUELESS
THE BOOK OF WHITE TRASH
THE ART OF MOONING
GOLFAHOLICS
CRINKLED 'N' WRINK LED
SMART COMEBACKS FOR STUPID QUESTIONS
YIKES! IT'S ANOTHER BIRTHDAY
SEX IS A GAME
SEX AND YOUR STARS
SIGNS YOUR SEX LIFE IS DEAD
40 AND HOLDING YOUR OWN
50 AND HOLDING YOUR OWN
MALE BASHING: WOMEN'S FAVORITE PASTIME
THINGS YOU CAN DO WITH A USELESS MAN
MORE THINGS YOU CAN DO WITH A USELESS MAN

THE WORLD'S GREATEST PUT-DOWN LINES
LITTLE INSTRUCTION BOOK OF THE RICH & FAMOUS
WELCOME TO YOUR MIDLIFE CRISIS
GETTING EVEN WITH THE ANSWERING MACHINE
ARE YOU A SPORTS NUT?
MEN ARE PIGS / WOMEN ARE BITCHES
THE BETTER HALF
ARE WE DYSFUNCTIONAL YET?
TECHNOLOGY BYTES!
50 WAYS TO HUSTLE YOUR FRIENDS
HORMONES FROM HELL
HUSBANDS FROM HELL
KILLER BRAS & Other Hazards Of The 50's
IT'S BETTER TO BE OVER THE HILL THAN UNDER IT
HOW TO REALLY PARTY!!!
WORK SUCKS!
THE PEOPLE WATCHER'S FIELD GUIDE
THE ABSOLUTE LAST CHANCE DIET BOOK
FOR MEN ONLY (How To Survive Marriage)
THE UGLY TRUTH ABOUT MEN
NEVER A DULL CARD
THE LITTLE BOOK OF ROMANTIC LIES
THE LITTLE BOOK OF CORPORATE LIES ($ 6.95)
RED HOT MONOGAMY ($ 6.95)
LOVE DAT CAT ($6.95)
HOW TO SURVIVE A JEWISH MOTHER($ 6.95)
WHY MEN DON'T HAVE A CLUE ($7.99)
LADIES, START YOUR ENGINES! ($7.99)

NO HANG –UPS–CASSETTES Retail $5.98
Vol. I: GENERAL MESSAGES (M or F)
Vol. II: BUSINESS MESSAGES (M or F)
Vol. III: 'R' RATED MESSAGES (M or F)
Vol. V: CELEBRI-TEASE